SPEAK WITH NO FEAR

WORKBOOK

Go from a nervous, nauseated, and sweaty speaker
to an excited, energized, and passionate presenter

An Interactive Companion to the Best-Selling Public Speaking Book

Mike Acker

Copyright ©2021, Mike Acker

All rights reserved. No part of this publication may be reproduced, distributed, or transmitted in any form or by any means, including photocopying, recording, or other electronic or mechanical methods, without the prior written permission of the publisher, except in the case of brief quotations embodied in reviews and certain other non-commercial uses permitted by copyright law.

Some names and identifying details have been changed to protect the privacy of individuals.

ISBN: 978-1-954024-16-8

ISBN: 978-1-954024-17-5

READ THIS FIRST

Thank you for investing in my book.

In appreciation, I'd love to give you a free gift.

THE 3X3 VIDEO COURSE

This course covers the "3 Classics" that are the basis of effective public speaking and the "3 Questions" that will help you write better speeches.

It's the foundation of my coaching and has helped hundreds of people gain clarity and direction in creating their speech.

Visit this link or use the QR code for your free gift:
https://content.mikeacker.com

TABLE OF CONTENTS

INTRODUCTION	1
START HERE	2
THE SEVEN STRATEGIES	7
UNCOVER & CLEAN THE WOUND	9
IMAGINE THE WORST	18
YOU BE YOU	26
SPEAK TO ONE	36
IT'S NOT ABOUT YOU	44
CHANNEL THE POWER	49
BE IN THE MOMENT	56
CONCLUSION	63
ABOUT MIKE ACKER	67
BOOK MIKE ACKER	69
ALSO BY MIKE ACKER	72

INTRODUCTION

Speak with no fear.

Does that sound impossible?

You've heard the statistics that say people are more afraid of public speaking than death. That doesn't mean we'd choose a firing squad over a podium. It means our fear of death is less pressing than our fear of speaking. In other words, death seems a long way off, but that Zoom presentation is in five days, seven hours, and nineteen minutes.

But there are some people who don't mind public speaking. They actually enjoy it. I know because I'm one of them. No, I wasn't born without adrenal glands. Nor was I always this way. In the Speak With No Fear book (SWNF), I share stories of my early struggles with public speaking, including the time I literally gave myself a psychosomatic fever to avoid facing my audience.

Learning to speak without debilitating fear is a skill that can be learned by anyone.

This workbook is designed to be a companion to Speak With No Fear. Download a preview of Chapter 3 at http://preview-wb.mikeacker.com. It complements the book with new tools and directed exercises. You can use this workbook by itself, but it contains only a fraction of the material found in the book, so I recommend using it side-by-side with SWNF. To download printable PDF worksheets for this workbook visit https://swnf-wb.mikeacker.com.

As you go through this workbook, you may be tempted to skip some of the questions and exercises. It is possible they don't actually apply to you. For instance, some of you won't need Strategy #1. But it's also possible you are avoiding it because of fear—some of you will really need Strategy #1 but will be reluctant to address your "speaking wound." It is also possible that those exercises have a value you don't yet see.

Here's my suggestion: Promise yourself to complete at least 25% of each question or exercise. If you want to stop after 25%, ask yourself "What's stopping me?"

If it's tedium, then skip it. If it's fear, press in harder. If it's insurmountable fear, set it aside for later.

Enough talk, let's get to work!

Mike Acker

START HERE

What is your proudest accomplishment? For the sake of this exercise, I'm not talking about relationship stuff. I mean something like running a marathon, getting your MBA, or writing a book. Something that required a lot of work. I mean, a lot. Like, people-thought-you-were-crazy-amount-of-work.

So, what is your big accomplishment?

_____

_____

I'm impressed. How much work did that take?

_____

_____

_____

No kidding. What motivated you to keep on going when you wanted to quit?

_____

_____

_____

I hear you. I woke up at 4:30 AM every morning for twenty-seven days straight to write SWNF. After working for a couple of hours, I'd get ready for my full-time job. Sometimes, it was fun. Sometimes, it was hard work. Sometimes, I just wanted to give up.

Why did I put so much effort into my book?

Because I wanted something in my life to change and that book was my ticket.

You probably know where I'm going with this. Learning to speak without fear will take work. This isn't called "Learn to Speak with No Fear in Your Sleep." You'll have to practice. You'll have to confront your fears. You'll have to be okay with making mistakes.

So, before we get started, I want you to create a clear picture of why it will be worth the work. Whenever you're tempted to set this workbook down in the middle of a difficult exercise, you can turn back to this chapter.

Start Here

THE SPEECH FAIRY

Let's pretend there is a magical Speech Fairy. I like to imagine he looks like The Rock in The Tooth Fairy. If you put the rough draft of your speech under your pillow, he'll replace it with a TED Talk worthy address and magically make you into a confident, engaging speaker.

Imagine you were just visited by the Speech Fairy. Do you feel different? What's the most immediate fear that's been lifted?

_____

_____

_____

Let's think longer term. How would your life change? Let's get real, and maybe a little selfish. Keep going until you have at least ten positive changes.

_____

_____

_____

_____

_____

_____

_____

_____

_____

_____

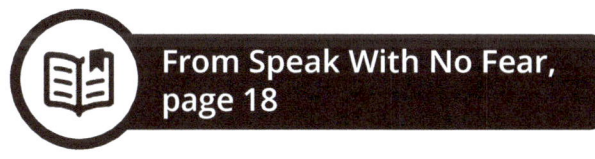

From Speak With No Fear, page 18

As you develop this public speaking skill, you will do better in your career. Don't overlook the value of improving your speaking skills. The famed investor, Warren Buffet, attributes part of his success to taking speaking lessons as a young man. The small actions you take here will translate to great actions out there in your world.

Public speaking is what I call a "universal advantage" – a skill that gives you an advantage in nearly any profession or situation. You could be a truck driver and your abilities as a speaker would still open up advancement opportunities. (Some of the other universal advantages include leadership, empathy, excellence, love of learning, and the ability to teach.)

THE BEST VERSION OF YOU

I forgot to tell you the Speech Fairy's one rule: He can't change your personality at all—he can only enhance what you already have. He can't turn an introvert into an extrovert or make you speak in a different octave. In fact (spoiler alert), all the Speech Fairy actually does is take the most comfortable version of you—you chatting freely with good friends over a coffee or beer—and puts that on stage.

Let's take a deeper look at this "chatting easily" you. Think back to last time that you had a great personal or professional conversation. You were engaged, the other person was engaged. You knew that you were giving them gold. Why did that conversation "work"? How did it feel?

_____

_____

_____

_____

The Speech Fairy is in the business of making that you into speaking you. Now, I want you to imagine what you will look and sound like after a visit from the Speech Fairy. I want details. What are you doing with your hands? Are you energetic as Reese Witherspoon or as steadfast as Morgan Freeman? What are you wearing?

_____

_____

_____

_____

Now imagine how it feels like. Really lean into it. Do you feel confident? Powerful? Happy?

_____

_____

_____

_____

Let's put this all together. Take everything you've written so far, and write out a personal vision statement. Begin with the words, "I'm going to be a public speaker who is..."

_____
_____
_____
_____

THERE IS NO TRY

Pause for a moment. Do you really believe you are capable of becoming that speaker?

From Speak With No Fear, page 28

In The Empire Strikes Back, Luke is training to become a Jedi knight when Yoda tells him to use the force to levitate his X-wing out of a swamp.

"Okay," Luke whines. "I'll give it a try."

Yoda responds with his iconic line: "Do. Or do not. There is no try."

Either you believe that you'll become a better speaker and do it, or you won't believe and will halfheartedly "try"—and fail.

What I'm saying is that "Just believe" is more than a Christmas-movie slogan. It is the only way forward because you won't put in the necessary effort if you don't genuinely believe.

Step out in courage. You can do this. You will do this. And each time you do, you will get better. Remember Mark Twain's words: "Courage is not the absence of fear, but the mastery of it."

So, what will it be, young padawan? Do, or do not? Write yourself a note right now saying why you believe that you can and *will* become that amazing speaker you just wrote about.

_____
_____

Start Here

_____

[blank lined writing space]

Let's make it official by making this pledge:

I, _____, am fully capable of becoming a great speaker—without becoming a different person. I will do the work and reap the rewards!

Signed: _____   Date: _____

Start Here

THE SEVEN STRATEGIES

01 Uncover & Clean the Wound

02 Imagine the Worst

03 You Be You

04 Speak to One

05 It's Not About You

06 Channel the Power

07 Be in the Moment

Start Here

01   Speaking with No Fear Strategy:
UNCOVER & CLEAN THE WOUND

Fair warning: This chapter requires courage and may push you further emotionally than you'd like. Most of us have created coping mechanisms for dealing with our past and things can get messy when we mess with them.

I am not a counselor and this advice is not a substitute for professional advice. If this chapter begins to feel unsafe, please set it aside and consult a mental health professional.

I've coached several hundred speakers and I've noticed a massive trend. Roughly two-thirds of my clients suffered from past speaking wounds that were still holding them back. I completely get that, because I'm part of the two-thirds.

Here is my story:

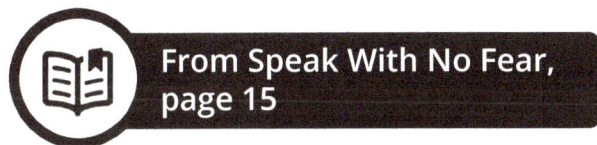
From Speak With No Fear, page 15

As a young child, I'd struggled with a speech impediment and was unable to pronounce the "j" sound. Fortunately, my parents were very proactive and purposeful speech therapy largely fixed the problem, though I still struggled at times. More importantly, that impediment instilled in me a slight hesitancy to talk aloud. By the time my family moved to Mexico in order to lead a non-profit organization, I had grown comfortable speaking English, but Spanish was another matter.

The day came when I had to give my first monthly presentation—in Spanish. La Maestra called me forward and all eyes were on me. Insecurity, doubt, and fear marked my interior. My nerves were fried before I reached the front. My stomach tightened as I opened my mouth because I knew what was coming: horrible, awful Spanish. Laughter started before I even finished my first sentence. Forty teenagers were laughing at me without restraint. I sped through my words to finish faster, making me sound funnier and less intelligible. La Maestra started laughing too. Finally, it was over and I rushed back to my seat.

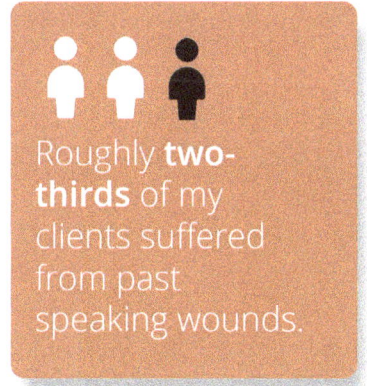
Roughly **two-thirds** of my clients suffered from past speaking wounds.

But it wasn't over. They continued teasing me the rest of the day and loudly mimicked my accented Spanish "behind my back." When the bell finally rang, I ran the entire three blocks to our house. The following morning, as I was dressing for school, fear gripped me again and I told my mom I was sick. She didn't believe me and took my temperature. Sure enough, I had a fever— psychosomatic sickness. I was literally sick with fear and never wanted to give another presentation in my life, let alone in another month.

Just about everyone experiences some level of fear of public speaking. That is normal.

But many people have an excessive fear driven by a speaking wound—a painful speaking event in your past that continues to affect you today.

> **Speaking Wounds may include:**
>
> - Parents or relatives who belittled or mocked some "public performance," even if it was just in the living room.
> - Classmates or teachers laughing at your presentation.
> - Having your personal value tied to how well you did on stage.
> - A work presentation that failed spectacularly and left you feeling like a failure.

Not sure if you have a "speaking wound"? Here's a quick test: When you think about giving a speech, do you experience a visceral fear that is disproportional to the situation?

Let's break that down.

- Visceral: Do you feel an immediate twist in your gut as if someone poked their finger in an open wound?
- Disproportional: Does your fear seem irrational, even to you?

If you answered yes, then keep reading. But if you're part of one-third who just feels a "normal" fear of speaking, feel free to skip to the next strategy.

Don't ruin **future successes** by ignoring **past pains**.

UNCOVERING THE WOUND

Time does not heal all wounds. In fact, infected wounds get worse over time. Unless you deal with your wound, it will continue to hijack your success.

When I work with clients and my normal strategies don't seem to reduce their fear, I ask if they have any painful speaking memories. Simply retelling the story uncovers the wound. As I said at the beginning, this is hard work, so let's start with some motivation.

If the Speech Fairy could magically heal your speaking wounds and remove your visceral fear, how would that feel?

_____
_____
_____
_____
_____
_____
_____
_____
_____
_____

How much work would that feeling be worth to you? What would you be willing to do to get it?

_____
_____
_____
_____
_____
_____
_____
_____
_____
_____

Okay then, let's get to work. What is your most humiliating speaking moment? Write it down without any judgment. Pretend you are telling a dear friend's story for them.

_____
_____
_____
_____
_____
_____
_____
_____
_____

I may not know you, but I'm proud of you. I'm serious—confronting the past is hard, hard work. But we aren't quite done. Using the following questions, make sure there aren't any other wounds to uncover.

- Have you been embarrassed in front of people? What happened?
- Did you ever get put on the spot without being ready for it? How did it turn out?
- Do you have memories of people making fun of you?
- Where have you fallen short of your own expectations?
- Why do you care so much about what people might think of you?

_____
_____
_____
_____
_____
_____
_____
_____

CLEAN THE WOUND

Do you know the difference between a scar and a wound? You can touch a scar without pain. That's our goal here. I want you to be able to look back on your speaking wounds without feeling so much as a twitch of anxiety. I believe that this section, combined with time, will allow you to do just that.

> **Note:** If you're a type A, intellectually driven person, this next exercise may seem too "touchy-feely," but I promise, it works. (Remember my 25% rule—humor me by completing 25% of it.)

Cleaning the wound begins with accepting yourself. That child, teenager, or adult that was wounded needs to be told that they are okay. They need to be told they weren't weak or stupid for how they felt. Write a letter to your younger self, telling them that you understand and that you accept them. Don't rush through this one.

_____

_____

_____

_____

_____

_____

_____

_____

_____

_____

_____

_____

How'd that feel? Hang with that feeling for a moment. Now reread this letter until you believe it. How do you feel now?

_____
_____
_____
_____
_____
_____

The next exercise is easier. I've discovered that almost all negative experiences can be used for good. Our pain can motivate us to grow and encourage others who have suffered through similar situations.

How can your speaking wounds motivate you to grow?

_____
_____
_____

How can your speaking wounds encourage others?

_____
_____
_____
_____
_____

#ProTip:

Name your speaking wound after the person who gave it to you. Start saying, "Knock it off, _____!" every time you feel the fear.

EXERCISE: TIME TO GIVE A SPEECH!

This last exercise is the biggest one yet. It's time to give a speech! Take everything you've learned so far and create a speech.

Here's a simple structure:

01 Introduction	02 Main Points	03 Conclusion

Introduction: Set the stage by sharing your journey of discovering your speaking wounds.

_____
_____
_____
_____
_____

Main points: Either briefly share your three main speaking wounds or else spend more time on the main one.

01
_____
_____
_____
_____

02
_____
_____
_____
_____

03 _____
_____
_____
_____

Conclusion: How you are moving on and not letting the past define your future. This is the lesson you want to bestow on others.

_____
_____
_____
_____

Giving Your Speech

Level 1: Great job. Now, give that speech to yourself in front of a mirror. Keep giving it until you feel comfortable.

Date completed: _____

Challenge exercise: Give this speech to a small group of friends.

Date completed: _____

Extreme exercise: Give this speech to a larger group, such as a civic group or at work.

Date completed: _____

Each time you give your speech, your wounds should hurt less, eventually becoming scars. If they don't—or if they get worse—then pain may be too deep for "self-help." I highly encourage you to find a counselor who can help you address your past pain.

With all the pain I faced living between two cultures and being bullied in the 9th grade, counseling has been an important part of my story. The words and actions of a few people left a mark on me that I hid for many years. I am grateful for how counseling helped me deal with the baggage I was carrying. Although it wasn't specifically about public speaking, the healing I experienced helped me accept myself, which led to increased confidence.

02 Speaking with No Fear Strategy: IMAGINE THE WORST

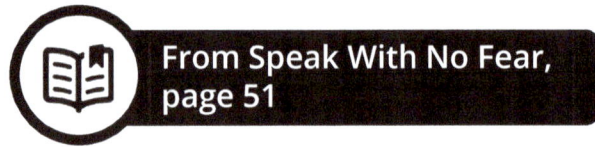
From Speak With No Fear, page 51

Think about sports, playing music, or any other type of performance. My sport growing up was soccer. Our practices didn't just simulate games; it exceeded them. At practice, we would run longer, take more shots, and confront greater challenges than in the games. Practices were never easy. They actually took an emotional toll on us. But we were ready when game time arrived. The coach had conditioned our bodies and minds for a grueling game. As a result, our games were easier than practice, and we usually conquered the other teams.

Can you relate? Did you put hours and hours into piano practice and, as a result, the recital went smoothly? Can you remember a time when you studied for weeks and aced the exam on the big day? We know this principle: the right kind of practice prepares us for the actual event. Or, as the Marines like to say, "The more you sweat in training, the less you bleed in battle."

"Imagine the Worst." Sounds like a pretty counterintuitive strategy, doesn't it? But imagining the worst when you're still "in practice" results in two huge, fear-destroying outcomes.

FIRST OUTCOME: CONTROLLING YOUR EMOTIONS

Think about your upcoming speech. If you don't have one, then either think about one you've given in the past or one you'd like to give someday.

Imagine it as fully as possible:
- Who will be there?
- Where will they be seated?
- Where will I stand?
- What will I be wearing?
- How many people are in the room?
- How big is the room?
- Will I have a microphone?
- Will I have a podium, lectern, music stand, or table in front of me?
- How long will my speech last?
- What mood will the people be in?
- What happens prior to my speech?
- What will happen after I speak?

Now imagine giving the speech. If you fully embrace this exercise, you should feel the stress and fear. In the movie *Click*, Adam Sandler's character gets a remote control that allows him to pause and fast forward time. Imagine you have that remote. The moment you feel afraid, pause your speech and answer this question:

What are you feeling right now? Where in your body are you feeling it?

_____
_____
_____
_____

Now hit play again but pause it as soon as the fear returns. This time you're going to practice calming yourself:

01	02	03
Take a deep breath. Now take another.	Smile (smiling has been shown to have many positive effects	Take a moment to notice five details in the room around you.

Great. Start the speech again, pausing to calm yourself when you feel the fear creeping up. How you practice now will impact how you do real life.

Date completed: _____

Let's take it up a notch. A lot of people practice in a "sterile environment" where there aren't any distractions and nothing goes wrong. But things do go wrong. A phone could ring in the middle of your big point. You could forget your notes, draw a complete blank, see people sleeping, or realize your zipper is down. You could accidentally drop an F-bomb to a group of old ladies.

EXERCISE: YOUR FIVE WORST CASE-SCENARIOS

I want you to write out your five worst case-scenarios.

01 _____

02 _____

03 _____

04 _____

05 _____

Imagine the Worst

Now, grab your magical remote and repeat the last exercise. Only this time, start imagining these things happening. Hit pause, work yourself through the calming techniques and then make notes on how you'll respond if it does happen.

01 Speaking disaster: _____

_____

My response: _____

_____

02 Speaking disaster: _____

_____

My response: _____

_____

03 Speaking disaster: _____

_____

My response: _____

_____

04 Speaking disaster: _____

_____

My response: _____

_____

05 Speaking disaster: _____

_____

My response: _____

_____

Date completed: _____

SECOND OUTCOME: REALIZING IT'S RARELY AS BAD AS YOU IMAGINE

Imagining the worst is about more than preparing for your emotions. It's also about getting proper perspective.

In 2019, I worked with JT, a confident and successful businessman. He'd started by launching one store and, over the course of a few years, expanded his business to 48 locations. In our coaching session, he was really struggling with a five-minute speech he had to give to the board of one of his competitors. He read it straight from his notes, seemingly afraid to look up from them.

"JT," I asked, "will you be nervous when you speak to this group?"

"Absolutely," he said. "Everyone sees me as confident, but when I'm in front of people, I get so nervous that I ramble."

"Why? What do you think is the worst thing that could happen?"

The question dove us into a hilarious dialogue about worst-case scenarios. The whole room laughs at him. His sweaty armpits cause the room to stink. Everyone starts cussing at him. Someone gets up and punches him.

JT wanted a great outcome from the speech, but he realized that his worst-case scenario wasn't that bad. Whatever happened, he'd be able to go home and be with his wife. He'd still have his job, his health, and his relationships. Realizing that took a lot of pressure off him and he was able to give a great speech—without anyone swearing or laughing at him.

Your turn. What are some of the worst things you could imagine happening to you? Someone yelling at you? Punching you? Someone writing an awful e-mail? Making a mistake that will damage your standing in the office? Think through five possibilities and how you'd respond.

_____

_____

_____

_____

We've already imagined your speech's worst-case scenarios. Now what about its best-case scenarios? Get a raise? Honor the bride and groom with your toast? Share your passion? Rewrite past fears? Inspire people to change? Gain respect and increase your value to the company?

_____
_____
_____
_____
_____
_____
_____
_____
_____
_____
_____
_____
_____
_____

EXERCISE: THE POSSIBLE GOOD OUTWEIGHS THE POSSIBLE BAD.

Human nature (aka survival instinct) is more inclined to dwell on the possible bad than good, so here's what I want you to do:

In the space below, write out as many possible good outcomes as you can under "PRO," leaving a space between each (you'll see why). Be very optimistic about what will happen if you do well. Visualize the best. Be detailed about the positives. Don't just write, "I could get a raise." Write down the exact amount you think you could get. Think about the positive emotions that people will experience. Be generous when you think about what good could come out of it.

Likewise, write out all the possible bad outcomes under "CON," being detailed about what could go wrong and leaving a speech between each. Just make sure you're as creative on the positive side of the page as you are with the negative.

PRO	CON
_____	_____
_____	_____
_____	_____
_____	_____
_____	_____
_____	_____
_____	_____
_____	_____
_____	_____
_____	_____

Now, go back and guestimate how long each of those pros and cons will remain with you and use the following notations in the lines you left blank:

- D: You'll forget about it the following morning.
- W: It will stick with you for a week.
- M: By the end of the month, it won't matter.
- Y+: It will still matter a year later.

Once you're done, read through the list again. Notice how the positives usually have a longer shelf life than the negatives. How does this exercise change your perspective on your speech?

_____
_____
_____
_____
_____
_____
_____

03 — Speaking with No Fear Strategy: YOU BE YOU

Writers talk about developing their "voice." What that means is that when we first start writing, we invariably sound like our favorite author. But the more we write, the more we sound like ourselves. This is also true of speakers.

From Speak With No Fear, page 66

That year, I embarked on a quest to discover "me" and my speaking voice, i.e., my style. I read books on speaking, and I listened to a few hundred sermons by other pastors. Each week, it seemed like I took on the personhood of the main podcast I listened to. One week, I was jovial and nonchalant like Rick Warren. The next week, I yelled a lot like Mark Driscoll and told people to repent. Then, I would become the famous black preacher TD Jakes (imagine a very white guy speaking to a small-town church trying to sound like TD Jakes!). I tried to be Joel Osteen, Rob Bell, Wes Davis, Andy Stanley, Kenton Beshore, Ed Young, and several others.

That congregation was in for a ride, but they were extremely patient. (Thank you!) Our church did grow a lot that year, perhaps partly because of the spectacle of which famous preacher the new kid would be imitating next.

As I tried on each identity, I struggled to find the real me. Then I watched this corny video called "U.B.U." (https://UBU.mikeacker.com, if you're interested.) Ed Young, one of the best-known pastors in America, recorded it for a conference to encourage speakers like me to stop trying to be someone else. That silly little video got through to me and I gave myself permission to be me.

Now go through this list and circle one attribute per line that best describes your ideal speaker:

Formal	or	Casual
Polished	or	Raw
Serious	or	Humorous
Intellectual	or	Relatable
Informational	or	Storyteller
Stoic	or	Emotional
Stationary	or	Constant Motion

We'll come back to this later, but I need to explain a crucial concept. Imagine you're about to give a speech but will be required to hold two five-pound dumbbells, at shoulder level, for the duration of your speech, but you can choose to hold them close to your chest or at arm's length.

Which would you choose?

The first weight represents the content of your speech. The better you know it, the closer you hold it to your chest. (If you're interested in how to create great content and internalize it, visit https://programs.stepstoadvance.com.)

The second weight represents your personhood. The more you are yourself, the closer you hold it to your chest. But the more you try to be someone else, the further out you hold it. Being someone else is exhausting!

AUTHENTICITY

Food Network Star was a reality TV show on the Food Network that was about finding (you guessed it) the next Food Network star. It starts with about a dozen aspiring chefs/stars and puts them through various challenges. One season, there was a chef who was very talented, but kept finding himself in the bottom two, narrowly avoiding being eliminated on a couple of occasions. His problem wasn't one of skill, but authenticity. The judges said he felt like a used car salesman. His mentor, Alton Brown, kept trying to get him to own his personhood. In one episode, the contestant casually mentioned that he used to be obese and had lost 200 pounds.

"You lost 200 pounds?" Brown asked, dumbfounded.

"Yeah," said the contestant. "That's why I care so much about cooking the way I do. It literally saved my life."

"Why am I just hearing about this?" Brown demanded.

"I don't like talking about it. It's very embarrassing."

What was happening? He was so afraid of being rejected that he put on a mask. But with a story like that, combined with his skills, he could have easily won. Instead, he was voted off that week.

Did you catch that? His inauthenticity didn't save him from rejection, it was the reason for it. The vast majority of audiences will accept you if you are yourself but reject you if you are not. Authenticity in speaking means giving your audience the real you, not the idealized, Instagram-ready version. This is not the same thing as "TMI"—willingly sharing anything and everything regardless of appropriateness.

Imagine you're about to give a speech that's deeply meaningful to you. You remember a personal story that would be very beneficial to your audience, but it's embarrassing and doesn't show you in the best light. How likely are you to tell it?

| Without hesitation | | With difficulty | | No way! |

Do you like your answer? If not, what steps should you take to change it?

_____
_____
_____
_____
_____
_____
_____

Resource:

Brené Brown has great books and talks about authenticity. If you struggle with being you, watch her TED Talk "The Power of Vulnerability" (brene.mikeacker.com).

WHAT MAKES YOU, YOU?

I've coached all kinds of speakers and have discovered that there is no "ideal speaking personality." Introvert or extrovert, charismatic or scholarly, it doesn't matter. Any personality type can be a great speaker—if they embrace their own personhood. It's time for another visit from the Speech Fairy. Remember his one rule? He can't change your personality, only enhance what you already have. His job is to help you fully be yourself on stage.

EXERCISE: YOUR SPEAKING ATTRIBUTES

Let's revisit the list of speaking attributes from earlier, but this time circle the attribute that best describes you:

Formal or Casual

O───────────O───────────O───────────O───────────O

Very Formal　　　　　　　　　In Between　　　　　　　　　Very Casual

Polished or Raw

O───────────O───────────O───────────O───────────O

Very Polished　　　　　　　　In Between　　　　　　　　　Very Raw

Serious or Humorous

O───────────O───────────O───────────O───────────O

Very Serious　　　　　　　　　In Between　　　　　　　　　Very Humorous

Intellectual or Relatable

O───────────O───────────O───────────O───────────O

Very Intellectual　　　　　　　In Between　　　　　　　　　Very Relatable

Informational or Storyteller

O───────────O───────────O───────────O───────────O

Very Informational　　　　　　In Between　　　　　　　　　Strong Storyteller

Stoic or Emotional

O───────────O───────────O───────────O───────────O

Very Stoic　　　　　　　　　　In Between　　　　　　　　　Very Emotional

Stationary or Constant motion

O───────────O───────────O───────────O───────────O

Fully Stationary　　　　　　　In Between　　　　　　　　　In Constant Motion

Now, have your significant other or a close friend describe you (cover your answers so you don't bias them):

Formal or Casual

Very Formal — In Between — Very Casual

Polished or Raw

Very Polished — In Between — Very Raw

Serious or Humorous

Very Serious — In Between — Very Humorous

Intellectual or Relatable

Very Intellectual — In Between — Very Relatable

Informational or Storyteller

Very Informational — In Between — Strong Storyteller

Stoic or Emotional

Very Stoic — In Between — Very Emotional

Stationary or Constant motion

Fully Stationaryl — In Between — In Constant Motion

Discuss any difference between your and their answers with them, then record what you learned about yourself:

_____
_____
_____
_____
_____
_____

Now go back and compare how you described yourself and your ideal speaker. What are three ways that you are like and unlike them?

_____
_____
_____
_____
_____
_____

What are five ways/situations where these differences can make you a better speaker than your ideal speaker? Don't stop until you have all five.

_____
_____
_____
_____
_____
_____

A QUICK NOTE ABOUT HUMOR

In *SWNF*, I talk a little more about humor and what comedians can teach you about embracing and using your personhood. Tina Fey and Robin Williams couldn't be more different, but both are funny.

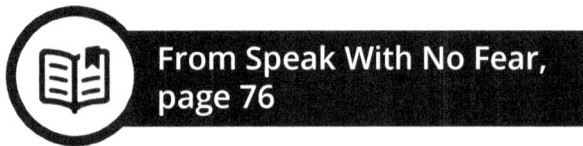

Done right, humor is one of the most powerful tools you have as a speaker. When you get people to laugh, they open up their hearts to you. If you can make them laugh, you can make them cry.

Here is what you need to understand: you are funnier than you realize.

I've often seen people do a negative metamorphosis when they begin their speech. I see jovial people become stoic, expressive people become robots, and confident people become timid. The "stage" can do something to people. It can make them act in ways unlike their usual self. In this metamorphosis, the first thing lost is humor.

STAGE PRESENCE

It's not just personality. Acting natural is more difficult than it sounds. Things you don't think about off stage—like what to do with your hands—suddenly requires much attention.

Begin by finding out what "acting natural" really means for you. Ask some of your friends to secretly record you in a casual conversation or two. Watch those videos and observe:

- Where do your eyes go?

- How often do you use your hands?

- What do you do with your hands when you're not talking?

- How deeply do you breathe?

- Are you quiet or loud? Speak fast or slow?

- Are you constantly moving or do you stay still? _____

- Do you smile or show a concerned face? _____

Record any other observations:

_____
_____
_____
_____
_____

This is you acting natural.

Now, either find a video of a past speech or record a new one in front of a mirror. Does that video reflect who you really are or did it feel artificial? What changes would you like to make?

_____
_____
_____
_____
_____

One last comment. On-stage you will always be a little different from off-stage you. For instance, you'll need to talk louder and use larger gestures. Said another way, on-stage you is just a bigger version of off-stage you.

YOU CAN IMPROVE YOU

Being yourself doesn't mean you can't grow or learn. In my speech program, I teach skills such as cadence, pace, dramatic pauses, and so on. I work with clients to increase their vocabulary, fluency, and presence. These are *improvements*, not *replacements*.

You can draw inspiration from great speakers without becoming them.

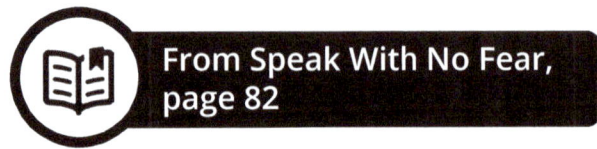 **From Speak With No Fear, page 82**

Don't just listen to one speaker, no matter how incredible they are or how much you connect with them. If you listen to one, you will become a clone. And don't just listen to two. Your attention will bounce back and forth. You will see the differences and you will get confused. Listen to three or more, and then you will see the peculiarities of each and be able to adopt certain skills as you identify your style.

- *Listen to one and become a clone.*
- *Listen to two and become confused.*
- *Listen to three or more and gain confidence by getting better.*

Intentionally watch comedians, news anchors, preachers, TED talks, and politicians. I often recommend Simon Sinek, Barack Obama, Ronald Reagan, Andy Stanley, and Ellen DeGeneres. Regardless of your religious or political views, these are great speakers who deliver with confidence.

Find at least three speeches/monologues and study them, watching them at least twice.

Record your observations:

Speech	Speaker	Notes

You Be You

Speech	Speaker	Notes

Challenge exercise: Study another three speeches.

Date completed: _____

Extreme exercise: Study three more speeches.

Date completed: _____

04 Speaking with No Fear Strategy:
SPEAK TO ONE

📖 **From Speak With No Fear, page 87**

The room had 3,200 seats that would soon be filled with a couple thousand people ready for me to talk about relationships. I stood on stage and did a quick rehearsal of my notes. I wanted to be ready, I wanted to be prepared, and I wanted my nerves to give positive energy and not to bring an anxiety attack. I envisioned the speech, did my mental exercises, and then I walked off the stage and prepared to meet people before the event started.

I met Georgia. She is a sweet grandmother whose son played for the Seattle Seahawks. Coming from Seattle, I knew who he was, and she was delighted to hear that.

I met Chad and we spoke for a bit. He was recently single and was trying to figure out the best steps ahead.

Tim and Sandy were a smiling couple who held hands while holding hot cups of coffee. They were recently married and had a spark of energy coming off of them.

Emily was a teenager. She was bubbly and a little bit nervous to talk to the speaker.

Isaac was fresh out of jail and needed to reboot his view on relationships. He was a bit skeptical, and yet was hoping to hear something that would inspire him and give him practical steps to take.

All the way up to when the event started, I stood out front and talked to people. I shook their hands. We introduced ourselves. Some of them were surprised (and even nervous) when they discovered I was the main speaker and was talking to them so casually. I learned a bit of their stories. They asked for a bit of mine.

As I chatted with all these people, the crowd dematerialized and became a bunch of individuals sitting next to each other to form a large audience. When I finally stood on stage, I was not speaking to a crowd but to Georgia, Chad, Tim, Sandy, Emily, and Isaac. I spoke to my new friends. I was excited to speak to them. I communicated my points to the audience as if I was speaking to those few that I knew.

I wasn't speaking into a faceless void; I was speaking into their lives.

This is one of the best, fear-crushing techniques I can give you: arrive early and get to know a handful of people from the audience, then focus on them as you speak. You can make a big room small by speaking to all as if you were speaking to one person (or more!) that you have personally connected with.

Forget the old "imagine your audience is in their underwear" technique. Imagine that the audience is filled with fully dressed friends. That will relieve fear.

Getting to know your audience is important for two reasons: 1) Your perception of the audience affects how you interact with them, which in turn affects how they treat you, and 2) Crowds increase fear, friends decrease it.

PERCEPTION AFFECTS RECEPTION

Think back to your nicest and meanest boss ever, then write their names here (feel free to use code if you're still working for the mean one!):

Nicest boss: _____

Meanest boss: _____

Now imagine your paycheck is missing ten hours of overtime and you have to confront your boss. Describe how that interaction would play out with each boss:

Nicest boss:

_____
_____
_____
_____
_____

Meanest boss:

_____
_____
_____
_____
_____

My point is that how we perceive our audience will directly affect both how we communicate with them and how enjoyable the experience will be.

The way you feel about your audience will come out in how you talk to them. Unless you're an Academy award-winning actor, it will seep out.

- *If you think they're stupid, you'll be condescending.*
- *If you think they dislike or are judging you, you'll be defensive.*
- *If you dislike them, you'll be rude.*
- *If you think they aren't worth your time, you won't be engaged.*
- *But, if you believe it's an honor to talk to them, you'll be grateful.*
- *If you genuinely like them and believe you have something worthwhile to give, you'll be excited.*
- *If you think they're awesome, they will be.*

...Your audience isn't stupid—they'll figure out how you feel about them. Their feelings towards you will be a mirror of your feelings towards them.

- *If you think they're stupid, they'll feel patronized.*
- *If you think they dislike or are judging you, they'll be defensive.*
- *If you dislike them, they'll want you to be done soon.*
- *If you think they aren't worth your time, they won't think you're worth their time and will tune you out.*
- *But, if you believe it's an honor to talk to them, they'll listen with open minds.*
- *If you genuinely like them and believe you have something worthwhile to give, they'll feel it and will physically lean in, ready to listen.*
- *If you think they're awesome, they'll think you're awesome!*

One more thing: Our survival instinct drives us to categorize nearly everything as a threat or ally. This means that it is all but impossible to approach your audience as neutral. You'll innately perceive them as either friends or foes. Friends decrease fear, foes increase it. Your goal, then, is to do everything you can to mentally view your audience as friends.

CROWDS VS. FRIENDS

Every time I speak in front of an audience, I remind myself that I am speaking to a person, not to a crowd. Crowds are scary. People are friends...

No. You are not speaking to a crowd; you are speaking to a person.

This is always my strategy. I always jump at any opportunity to personally and intimately connect with my audience beforehand. I don't want to speak to a crowd. I want to add value, educate, inform, entertain, and instruct people.

What's the difference between a crowd and a large group of people? A crowd is a single entity with a collective mind, and a group of people is a collection of individuals with different opinions and desires.

Learning to view your audience as a group of individuals makes them incredibly less scary. Try this exercise: find some way to observe a crowd—go to a game, attend a church service, watch a video online, or even just look at a picture.

Now imagine that you have to give a speech to that crowd. How do you feel?

_____
_____
_____
_____
_____
_____

Next, focus on a section of the crowd and choose five people and pretend they are friends of yours. Based only on what you can observe, make up backstories, give them names, and reasons for being there.

Imagine again giving a speech to that crowd but, this time, focus on those five people. Do you feel any different this time?

_____
_____
_____
_____
_____
_____
_____

I understand that for many of you, the thought of introducing yourself to strangers and getting to know your audience is scary, but hopefully you're starting to see why not doing so is even scarier.

In the next section, we'll address two objections to this strategy. Then, I'll give some practical tips via my personal "pre-meeting checklist." But for now, record why getting to know your audience is important, then make a personal commitment to do so:

___

___

___

___

___

OBJECTIONS:

 I'm an introvert.

Many of the best speakers I know are introverts, so I need to clarify something. Being introverted is not the same thing as being shy; in fact, there are many non-shy introverts. The introverted/extrovert scale describes how you respond to social interaction. Mark where you are on the scale below.

Does being with two or more people drain or energize you?

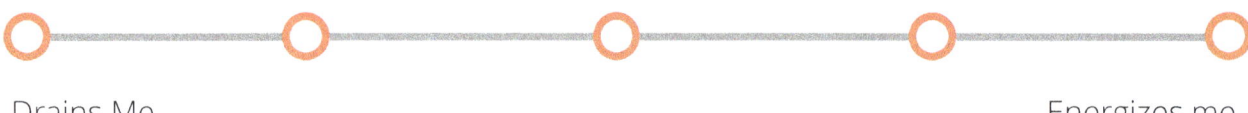

Drains Me   Energizes me

The closer you are to the "Drain" side of the scale, the more introverted you are.

If you're extroverted, then this strategy will be easier for you. Talking to the audience beforehand will probably amp you up! This still works for introverts, but it'll just take more work.

Here are my suggestions:
1. Conserve your "social bandwidth" by not doing anything too social in the days prior to your speech and
2. Give yourself permission to spend more time with fewer people. And if you're shy? Then this may be even harder, but still worth the effort.

02 It's a Zoom/teleconference meeting.

The COVID pandemic was a catalyst for widespread adoption of virtual communication, so it's very likely some of your speeches will not be done in front of a live audience. Try these two techniques:

First, do your research.

Whenever I prepare to meet a prospective client or for a virtual meeting, I use LinkedIn, Twitter, Facebook, and Instagram to find out who they are. I visit their websites and read their blogs. In this day and age, there is seldom an excuse for going into any meeting or presentation blind.

Second, if you aren't able to research your audience, use the exercise we used at the beginning of this strategy: **try to imagine who they are**—create three characters with backstories and speak to those personal connections in the audience.

MY PRE-MEETING CHECKLIST

1. **ARRIVE EARLY AND PREPARE EARLY.**

Lack of preparation creates stress and prevents you from connecting with your audience.

Carefully backward engineer your departure time:
- How much time do you need to travel to the event?
- Now think through all the logistics and preparation:
- Familiarize yourself with the space and conduct a rehearsal.
  - All audio and visual set up (mic check, test slides, etc).
  - Room setup: props, pictures, tables and chairs, booklets, merchandise, food, etc (never assume it will be done for you or that it will be done to your standards!)
- How much time will all these things take? Assume everything will take longer than it should.
- Now add an additional hour for meeting people and add all these times together. That is how much lead time you need.

When you prepare the space, you **create peace.**

#ProTip:

Always print two copies of your notes. Even if one is electronic, print another. Trust me, you'll sleep better.

2. DON'T DRINK COFFEE OR ENERGY DRINKS WHILE YOU ARE WAITING ESPECIALLY IF YOU'RE NERVOUS.

Sugar and coffee temporarily and artificially increase energy. When you're anxious, you already have nervous energy flowing through your body. Combine the negative energy of fear with the amped-up energy of caffeine and sugar, and your senses will overload.

3. STAND WHERE YOU CAN MEET A FEW PEOPLE.

Often, a speaker will stand apart from the audience. Don't do that. Get in there with the people. I have a simple rule.

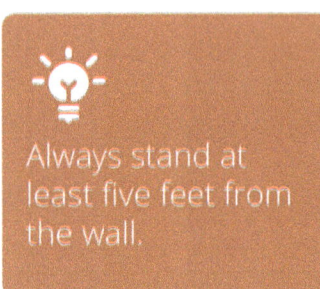

Always stand at least five feet from the wall.

Most people like to "hide" by the wall and take cover behind cell phones or coffee cups. Embrace this rule and people will feel like you are embracing them. It also exudes confidence because it shows you're not a wallflower that needs to hide.

#ProTip:
Never pass up on the opportunity to eat with your audience.

4. SMILE.

From Speak With No Fear, page 102

Why? Because smiling enhances your attractiveness, which also enhances your confidence.

Smiling is a natural antidepressant. The act of smiling enhances the way your neural communication functions, and it releases neuropeptides along with dopamine and serotonin.

Smiling reduces your blood pressure. Try it! Go to the store and sit at one of those little tables that take your blood pressure. Then smile for a full minute and try again.

Smiling boosts your immune system!

Smiling alters your brain chemistry, decreases your nerves, and strengthens your voice—and your audience will feel it.

Smiling connects you to other people.

Smiling relaxes your audience and encourages them to smile back.

I can't stress this enough. It is the number one advice I give. Smile.

5. MAKE IT YOUR MISSION TO CONNECT WITH 3-5 PEOPLE.

You can meet more, but create a connection with three to five people. It's not enough to know their names. Forget for a moment that you are going to communicate to people and work to connect with people. Knowing who you are as an extrovert or an introvert, commit now to how many people you'll connect with before your next speech:

Do these things then you'll be speaking to people and not a crowd. Whether it's 10 or 100 or 1000 people in the room, find your new friends and talk to them.

And don't forget to smile.

MY PRE-MEETING CHECKLIST

(Go to content.mikeacker.com for a printable version)

- I will ensure that I finish all preparation at least an hour before my speech.
- I will arrive early.
- I will not get hyped on coffee or sugar.
- I will stand away from the wall to meet people.
- I will smile.
- I will connect with 3-5 people.
- I will not be worried; I will stay in the moment with people.
- I will speak to PEOPLE, not to the crowd.
- I will be okay.

05 Speaking with No Fear Strategy:
IT'S NOT ABOUT YOU

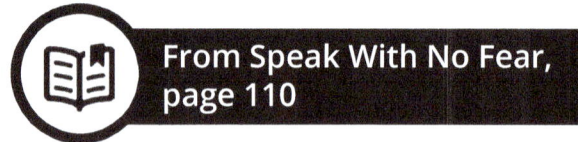 From Speak With No Fear, page 110

In the movie What Women Want, starring Mel Gibson and Helen Hunt, Mel's character is a stereotypical male chauvinist who suddenly gains the power to hear what women are thinking. In one scene, Mel pitches his idea in the boardroom, but as he "works" his message, he is struck by the discovery that, even though everyone is looking at him, the women are focused on their own concerns. Their eyes are on him; their thoughts are not.

What Mel experienced in the movie is the reality we face each time we talk to a group—people are far less concerned about you than you fear.

Think about the last presentation you attended. What percentage of your thoughts were about the speaker? Like you, I've been in the audience for many different types of presenters: comedians, salespersons, preachers, teachers, leadership gurus, coaches, valedictorians, and a myriad of others. While I try to think about the content of their words, I've often been swept away by a wide variety of thoughts: "Will this be helpful to me? I like math more than biology. I should plan my upcoming vacation. He looks so confident...I wonder what I look like. Shoot—my fly is down!" And so on.

When you focus on yourself, you'll find every flaw.

Do you see what I'm saying? While the presenter is often afraid of what people think about them, the audience is more concerned thinking about themselves.

Unless you're a narcissist, knowing this will free you up and allow the pressure of the moment to fade.

Next time you listen to a speech, observe how often your mind is—and isn't—on the speaker and answer the following questions.

What percentage of the time you were actively thinking about:

The speaker themselves: _____

Their message: _____

Something else: _____

Now take it a bit further. When was your attention most drawn to the speaker:

And when was it drawn to his/her message:

Based on my experience, the less self-conscience a speaker is and the more he/she is focused on their audience, the less the audience notices the speaker and the more attention they pay to the message.

How do you think not focusing on yourself will help you speak with less fear?

One more question about being in the audience. Were you rooting for the speaker or hoping they fail?

That's right. Unless you have some sort of grudge against the speaker, you want them to succeed. Not just because you aren't a sociopath, but also because if they succeed in giving a good speech, you succeed in learning, growing, or being entertained.

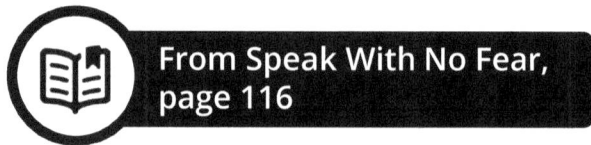
From Speak With No Fear, page 116

If you stand on stage and focus on how well you are doing, then you will be nervous, concerned, and fearful. You will feel like everyone is thinking of you, judging you, and critiquing you. Remember, just because all eyes are on you does not mean that all the attention is on you. They see you and they hear you, but they are thinking of themselves. Shift your focus. Think about them. How can you help them? How can you instruct them? How can you lift them up? How can you educate them? How does your pitch serve them?

"GIVE AND IT SHALL BE GIVEN TO YOU"

Here is the irony of public speaking: The more you focus on giving your audience what they want, the more you will get what you want. When you consistently do this, you'll develop a great reputation and achieve your goal. But be careful. People are very perceptive and they can tell when you are manipulating them. Think back on experiences you've had with commissioned salespeople. Have you been able to tell which ones pretended to care about your needs and which ones actually did? How?

___

___

___

___

___

In my "3 Questions" teaching video (available for free at https://content.mikeacker.com), I teach the Why, What, and Who of speaking. I want you to focus on the second two—what does your audience want and who are they?

Imagine giving a five-minute speech on "What I do for a living" for each of the following groups. How would your presentation change in each scenario?

High school students at a job fair:

___

___

___

Fellow professionals at a "meet and greet":
_____
_____

Your local senator and her staff:
_____
_____

Third graders in your nephew's class:
_____
_____

Notice how much the content of your speech shifts based on who your audience is and what the meeting is about.

Now imagine your next speech and think carefully about the Who and What. Don't skimp on this exercise. It is the foundation on which your speech will be built. Do your job here, and your presentation will be audience-focused and well-received, which in turn will lower your fear. But fail here and your speech could be a train wreck. Don't believe me? Imagine mixing up your notes from that last exercise and giving the wrong speech to each group.

Who is your audience? It's your job as a speaker to carefully study them so you can serve them. Include items such as age, gender, profession, education level, religious or political background, and familiarity with your topic.
_____
_____
_____
_____

Based on the above data, what sort of adjustments might you need to make to both the content and presentation of your speech?
_____
_____
_____
_____

What do they want to gain from your talk? Why are they having you speak to them? How can you help, serve, entertain, inform, educate, or inspire them?

_____

_____

_____

_____

Let's take it even deeper. Try to get into their heads and ask:

What are their hopes and dreams?

_____

_____

What are their fears?

_____

_____

What do you have that you can give them? (Motivation, tips, information, laughter…)

_____

_____

06 Speaking with No Fear Strategy: CHANNEL THE POWER

 From Speak With No Fear, page 133

Have you ever listened to a knowledgeable but boring speaker? Maybe it was a tenured professor who clearly preferred the library to the lecture hall or a pastor who never looked up from his notes or varied his tone. They probably knew their content very well and may have even been experts in their field. They regularly speak in front of their church, classroom, co-workers, or the organization they started. These boring communicators take the audience for granted. They assume the audience is interested just because they're present. They just work to give you their content, not to connect.

Do you know what their problem is? They truly "speak with no fear." They have stopped caring about the outcome. They became complacent.

> The goal isn't to eliminate fear but to channel it into positive energy.

One reason why you are worried, scared, nervous, or terrified is because you care. You care about doing well. You care about getting your message across. You care about what people think.

Time to be honest, the title "Speak With No Fear" is intentionally misleading.

I've spoken hundreds upon hundreds of times, but I'm proud to say that I'm still nervous *every* time and I never want that to change. It's my edge. If I ever erased my fear, then I'd eliminate the energy that makes me interesting.

Think of a time when fear of failing—a test, a recital, a job—drove you to work harder.

How would have the outcome been different if you didn't care?

_____

_____

_____

The problem isn't fear, but debilitating fear. The goal of this strategy is teaching you how to redirect your fear and convert it from a destructive force into one of your greatest assets. Don't eliminate your nervousness, channel it.

Take a moment to think of your public speaking fear. Now that you're almost 75% of the way through this workbook, how has your fear changed? Can you see how it can be an asset?

___

___

___

___

From Speak With No Fear, page 138

The Grand Coulee Dam extends 550 feet high and 500 feet wide. It holds approximately 2,377,500,000,000 gallons of water—that's a lot of dam water!

The water is channeled into the penstocks—massive pipes that carry the water to the huge turbines. The water's force is captured by hydroelectric power-generating units that produce enough electricity to power every household in Washington State. That's a lot of dam power! (Sorry, last one.)

If the Grand Coulee Dam were to break, the damage would be unimaginable, causing destruction as far away as Portland, Oregon, 600 miles downstream. It is only by controlling the flow of water that a dam can be harnessed for good.

In the same way, a river of energy is building up in your reservoir as you prepare for your speech. Nervousness, stress, chaotic care, fear, and anxiety are splashing around inside of you.

Don't eliminate it and become complacent or boring, certainly. But don't let it all out at the same time either and release all your energy in a torrent of nervous energy. Your audience will drown in your flood of words and information. That is what happened in my college speech from Strategy #2. A surge of words were released but none were remembered.

The trick is controlling your energy, using these three penstocks that allow you to slowly release your nervousness and direct your dam energy. (Couldn't resist.)

Here are six penstocks you can use right now to capture and direct your energy. The first three focus primarily on your pre-speech energy and the second three on your mid-speech energy.

PENSTOCK #1: PREPARATION

Whenever you feel nervous energy stirring in you, immediately channel it into preparation. Write out your speech. Create note cards. Practice it in your mind. Practice in front of the mirror. Practice to anyone who will listen. Practice with a coach and let him/her critique you. Rewrite the speech. Put it on new note cards and practice it again.

Effort is energy at work. As you direct your "effort energy" towards your preparation, you will have less anxious energy distracting you.

#ProTip:

The first time you give the speech should never be the first time you say the speech:

- Attend speech workshops such as Toastmasters, the Dale Carnegie Institute, or my public speaking programs.
- Hire a coach to give you feedback.
- Invite friends to listen to you.
- If you're part of a church or club, look for smaller groups where you can share in front of others.

PENSTOCK #2: PREEMPTIVE EXERCISE

Hit the gym. Take a run. Go for a walk. Get your blood pumping and the energy flowing. If you use lots of your energy for physical exertion, you will have less energy for emotional exhaustion. I'm not just talking about the day I speak—I have a full routine that I follow the week before every big speaking engagement:

Pre-speech exercise routine

5 days before:	Normal exercise level
4 days before:	Normal exercise level
3 days before:	Light workout. Eat extra healthy.
2 days before:	Go big! Exhaust yourself and eat healthy.
1 day before:	Rest. Eat healthy.
Day of:	Do a light workout and focus on stretching. Eat healthy, but make sure you eat. Do NOT skip!

PENSTOCK #3: POWERFUL BREATHING

Most people fail to breathe enough. There are books and blogs on why deep breathing is important and how to breathe. Ultimately, deep breathing works.

Taking time to breathe deeply restores you at a cellular level. It calms you from the core of your being. Deep breathing is correlated with peacefulness, stillness, and calmness. Conversely, short breaths are characteristic of panic attacks. Turn your panic into peace by learning to breathe deeply.

Practice breathing deeply several days before your event so you're ready to perform deep breaths the day of. I am not a health expert and this isn't medical advice, but here is a basic breathing exercise that works for me:

1. Sit in a comfortable position.
2. Place one hand on my chest and another on my stomach.
3. Close my eyes.
4. Breathe in through my nose.
5. Be mindful that my belly pushes my hand out (chest remains still.)
6. Breathe out through open lips.
7. Take note of my belly going in.
8. Repeat 6 more times.
9. Be aware of my body and breathe.
10. Open my eyes and smile.

PENSTOCK #4: PAUSES

Purposeful pauses are powerful. Like the white space that graphic artists intentionally put into their designs, pauses create a void which the audience fills with their attention. Audiences will lean in to hear what is on the other side of the…

… pause.

Pauses also allow you to take a deep breath. Pauses allow you to control the torrent of words. Pauses allow you to regain composure. Pauses allow you to be present.

Find a speech you can practice. Ideally your next speech or a past one. Otherwise, you can find a speech online. Now give that same speech, or sections of it, to yourself multiple times. Each time, experiment with pausing at different spots: At the end of a paragraph, before a big point, after a big point, in the middle of a sentence, try it all.

What did you learn about the power of purposeful pauses?

_____

_____

_____

_____

PENSTOCK #5: PURPOSEFUL MOVEMENT

Never pace the stage. Those who pace do so out of unharnessed nervousness. It is distracting and obnoxious. Instead, direct that energy into purposeful movements.

Take that same speech from the last exercise (you should really know it by now!) and give it to yourself several more items, this time experimenting with different types of movements: standing still, pacing, moving to a different spot with each point, moving forward to emphasize something. Video the entire thing.

First, record how the different types of movements felt as you did them.

_____

_____

_____

_____

Now, watch the video. How did the different movements look?

_____
_____
_____
_____
_____

What did you learn from this exercise? What sort of purposeful movements do you want to use to channel your energy?

_____
_____
_____
_____
_____

PENSTOCK #6: PLANNED PASSION

Controlling your energy doesn't mean getting rid of it but converting and directing it. Convert it into *passion* about what really matters.

> "Light yourself on fire with passion, and people will come from miles to watch you burn."

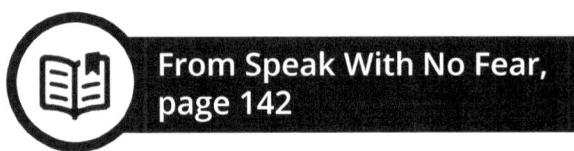

From Speak With No Fear, page 142

This is what we feel in Martin Luther King Jr.'s "I Have a Dream" speech or JFK's, "Do not ask your country what it can do for you, but what you can do for your country." This is what we see in Billy Graham, Steve Jobs, Oprah Winfrey, John Maxwell, Bill and Melinda Gates, Anderson Cooper, Craig Groeschel, TD Jakes, Preacher Lawson, and any number of other speakers who grab your attention.

This can be you.

You don't have to be a president, a CEO, a famous preacher, or a TV host. You just have to have the energy of caring.

Care about the message.

Care about the people you are giving it to.

Care about the content of your words. It doesn't matter if it's a wedding toast, business proposal, presentation to your coworkers, interview, or detailed report to your boss, so long as it matters to you.

This is the "why" question from Strategy 5: Why do you care about this topic? You must be able to answer that question because, if you don't care, your audience won't either.

Why do you really, truly, deeply care about your topic?

_____

_____

_____

_____

But one important principle: Don't put 100% of your passion into 100% of your presentation. If everything is important, then nothing is. Instead, purposely plan which parts of your speech are really important. Be passionate about those parts.

Don't avoid passion—direct all of the negative energy of fear into the positive energy of passion!

07 Speaking with No Fear Strategy
BE IN THE MOMENT

From Speak With No Fear, page 152

When I was 5, I wanted to be 10. When I was 15, I wanted to be 16. When I was 16, I wanted to be 18. When I was 18, I wanted to be 21. When I was 21, I wanted to be 25.

Now that I've passed 40, I want to be 25.

Can you relate? When you were younger, you wanted to be older. Now that you are older, you want to be younger. The irony! We often want to be a different age than we are. In life, we get so anxious wanting to be somewhere else that we forget to be where we are.

My guess is that, right now, you want to be on the other side of your speech. You just want to "get this over with." Just like being so eager to get older that you couldn't enjoy being younger, being in a hurry to get past your speech will cause you to miss out.

There are three basic stages of a speech: preparation, presentation, and reflection. Don't be in a hurry to get to the next one; enjoy, embrace, and learn from each.

FIRST STAGE: PREPARATION.

In preparation, you'll research content and develop speaking skills. I really enjoy this stage! I get to learn and grow. Preparing for your speech, presentation, or talk is a journey and, with a little bit of planning, you'll be able to get the most out of it.

Research Content: Never start writing your speech at the last moment. Start at the first moment and give yourself unstructured time to learn for the sake of learning. What are five things you'd like to learn as you write your next speech?

_____
_____
_____
_____

What are some of the best resources for researching your topic?
_____
_____
_____

Now set aside a frivolous amount of time to explore. Forget about your speech and just enjoy learning.

Date completed: _____

Develop skills

This technique is straight from the Toastmasters manual. Regardless of the speech's topic, a toastmaster is expected to work on a specific skill with each speech, such as pausing purposefully or using visual aids.

List five specific speaking skills that you want to develop:

_____
_____
_____
_____
_____

With each new speech you give (even if it's the same speech given five times), choose one of these skills to focus on. Do some research and watch videos of speakers who excel at that technique.

SECOND STAGE: PRESENTATION

From Speak With No Fear, page 116

In the TV show The Voice, super-star musicians coach their contestants through a series of performances in hopes of seeing them voted to the top. These coaches' top qualification isn't having the most talent—in fact, they'll often say that their contestants have better voices than them. What they have is experience.

What's the number one piece of advice that these veterans give to their singers just before they go up on stage?

"Have fun!"

On the surface, that seems so trite, like something you'd say to a seven-year-old going to play t-ball. But on one occasion, Pharrell explained that having fun on stage is infectious. If the performer has fun, so will the audience. By focusing on enjoying the moment, the contestant would be able to ignore the fear and give the audience what they really wanted.

Focus on the fun, not the fear.

Fear and joy are mutually exclusive emotions. If you are able to focus on having fun, your fear will dissipate.

Be in the moment. Enjoy this. Have fun!

This is it. After all the preparation, it's time to give your speech, toast, presentation, or Zoom seminar. Just like Pharrell talking to one of his young singers on The Voice, these are my last words to you before you start:

Imagine yourself giving your next speech.

You are on the stage and you've already:
- Cleaned your speaking wounds,
- Prepared for the worse,
- Practiced being yourself,
- Become friends with one or two people in the audience,
- Created great, audience-centered content that you're eager to share, and
- Channeled your negative energy into positive energy.

See yourself talking confidently and being free from debilitating fear. How do you feel in that moment?

_____
_____
_____
_____
_____

I hope you said things like excited, energized, empowered. I hope you feel honored to serve your audience. This is the moment I want you to embrace.

IT'S A CONVERSATION

A speech is not a monologue, it's a conversation. You may do all the talking, but the audience is still communicating with you. In one-on-one conversations, we can tell when someone checks out. If you are not fully present when you speak, then you'll miss what you can learn from your audience. Don't rush to the finish line. Stay in the moment. Notice what people react to. Watch what makes them nod and when they look bored. Use your energy to energize them.

Think through a recent speech. What are some of the ways your audience communicated with you without using words?

_____
_____
_____
_____
_____

How can you respond to what they "tell" you?

_____
_____
_____
_____
_____

#ProTip:

Some people's "listening expression" is a blank face. Don't let them throw you off. Find some expressive people to focus on instead.

speech, let alone during the middle of a speech. However, you can reiterate or explain things that seem to confuse your audience or abbreviate things they seem to understand more quickly than anticipated.

Other than that, there are three simple adjustments I recommend during the speech:

1. Gently roll your shoulders back.
2. Take a deep breath.
3. Smile!

TODAY, YOU ARE GIVING THE SPEECH!

Relax. Are you ready? At this point, it doesn't matter.

Did you do all the exercises? Maybe, who cares? You can't change that.

Do you know your speech? You have notes. You know as much as you know. Smile. Will others do better? Maybe. Probably. Forget about them. You be you.

Are people going to enjoy your presentation? Hopefully. Do your best. Leave the rest.

Can you help the audience? Yes. You are here for this group. Speak to them.
Is failure possible? Not right now. Don't worry about later. You can't change it.
Should you have changed your speech? No "should've, would've, could've." Drop it.
What could you do differently right now? Nothing. So be fully present.

The past cannot be changed.
The future is not determined.
This is now.
This moment is your present.
Receive it like the gift that it is.

THIRD STAGE: REFLECTION

The speech is done. You were present. You connected. You're exhausted. And now the doubts kick in. You realize all the things you forgot to say. Listen very carefully to this hard-won wisdom: Whatever happened, happened. Enjoy your moment and don't dwell on anything negative the day of the speech. The following day, once you're emotionally separated but the memory is still fresh, turn back to this page.

We often complete any given task, only to immediately move onto the next. This fails to relish our victories or learn from our failures. This happens in public speaking as well. Embrace the reflection stage. Be in the moment. This is what separates the amateurs from the pros.

The amateurs say, "Wow, I'm so glad to be done with that!" without realizing that taking time to reflect will grant insights into both the content communicated and the connection created with the audience.

The pros intentionally examine their performance and evaluate what worked and what didn't. They are able to look at themselves dispassionately in order to learn, not judge.

Step out of yourself and pretend that you've been hired to coach the speaker. Even if you only have five minutes, do a Celebrate—Cut—Change (CCC) of your speech. Even better, record your speech and watch it at this point. It doesn't matter if it's a simple work presentation, a school speech, a wedding toast, or a high-level engagement. Relive the moment so that you can learn from it.

Celebrate: What did you do well? What worked? Make note so you can repeat it.

_____
_____
_____
_____
_____
_____

Cut: What didn't work? What do you need to avoid? Make note of that as well so you *don't* repeat it.

_____
_____
_____
_____
_____

Change: What could be better next time? What can you edit? Write down three areas to improve. Not thirty—it's very hard to work on thirty different things.

_____
_____
_____
_____
_____

> Challenge exercise: Repeat the above exercise with a trusted friend.
>
> Date completed: _____
>
> Extreme exercise: Repeat the above exercise with some people known for their insight, if not tact.
>
> Date completed: _____

CONCLUSION

 From Speak With No Fear, page 173

I've tried CrossFit twice. The first time, I hit it hard. I was in the gym four or five times per week, putting in a full workout. I gave it my all. Soon after I joined, people remarked on the development of my shoulders. I noticed my shrinking stomach. I worked hard and it showed.

Then, my wife and I moved to California. Work picked up, and I tried to join CrossFit again, but I created excuses for why I couldn't show up all the time. I improved a bit, but not enough to get noticed. I didn't work hard—and it showed.

In the second scenario I could blame the gym, but the reality was I simply didn't do the work.

Throughout my years of coaching people, there is one constant. Our returns are determined by our investment. Choose to invest in yourself.

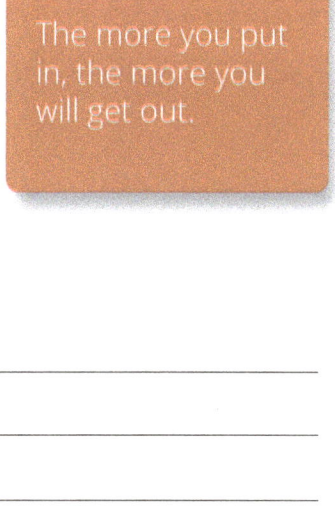

The more you put in, the more you will get out.

Almost done now. Sort of. I want you to go back to the Introduction and reread all your answers. Reflect on your journey and how you've grown.

_____
_____
_____
_____
_____
_____
_____
_____
_____

EXERCISE: REVIEW

Let's now reflect on the Seven Strategies. Under each one, summarize it in your own words and assess your current competence in it:

1. Uncover & Clean the Wound
   _____
   _____

2. Imagine the Worst
   _____
   _____

3. You Be You
   _____
   _____

4. Speak to One
   _____
   _____

5. It's Not About You
   _____
   _____

6. Channel the Power
   _____
   _____

7. Be in the Moment
   _____
   _____

Conclusion

Now rank them, giving a "1" to the one you are weakest at, then working your way down to "7."

___ Uncover & Clean the Wound

___ Imagine the Worst

___ You Be You

___ Speak to One

___ It's Not About You

___ Channel the Power

___ Be in the Moment

SET A DATE

Here's my suggestion. Pull out your phone or planner and map out one hour to work on the strategy you marked "1." Put it on your calendar now. Don't push it off too far.

Once you schedule it, make sure you show up to this important meeting with yourself. Then, schedule the next one. For best results, schedule one hour every day for five days. After all, it's just like the gym: the more you put in, the more you will get out.

Continue working on that strategy until it moves to the bottom of the list. Then, tackle the next highest.

ONE LAST ENCOURAGEMENT

 From Speak With No Fear, page 177

In the movie 8 Mile, superstar rapper Eminem plays the part of B-Rabbit, but many of the movie's events were based on his own life and own struggles to be successful. The movie featured the song "Lose Yourself," which won the Academy Award for Best Original Song—the first rap song to ever do so. The song basically asks the question, "If you only had one chance to get what you wanted, would you take it?"

The moment you used to dread—you're now facing your fears—is coming. When it comes, embrace it. You'll only have it once.

Lean in. Be present. Act on the strategies. Discard your worries. Speak to one. Remember that it is not about you. Do the work. Enjoy the process. Be here now.

You can do this.

Others have done this. I've worked with people just like you and fear no longer controls them.

Simply start doing what you need to do in order to get where you want to be. You won't erase your fear—not in one day or one week or one month—but you will ease your fear. You will learn to channel that nervousness into an engaging presence. You will do great. You really will.

You don't have to live in fear any longer.

ABOUT MIKE ACKER

Mike Acker is a keynote speaker, author, and executive and communication coach with over twenty years of experience in speaking, leadership development, and organizational management.

Known for his authenticity, humor, and engaging presence, Mike specializes in fostering personal and organizational awareness, allowing clients to create their own personal growth track. His approach is earnest, informed, and holistic, leading to a more satisfying balance in work and life. His expertise in communications and leadership has attracted politicians, business entrepreneurs, educational leaders, and executive managers.

Mike has been a professional speaker for over twenty years and has spoken to groups of 10 to 10,000. His training stretches from private Spanish schools in Mexico, to national college debate tournaments, master classes in cultural leadership, and certifications in coaching.

As a believer in giving back, Mike has worked with and supported several non-profits and relief organizations. Most recently, he served as the board chairman for GO on the Mission, an international non-profit working to lift kids out of poverty in Senegal and Mexico. (https://www.goonthemission.com.)

Mike also enjoys rock-climbing, wake surfing, skiing, church, building Legos with his son Paxton, and going on dates with his wife Taylor. Mike believes in the power of prayer, exercise, journaling, and real community to counter the stresses of everyday life.

www.mikeacker.com

BOOK MIKE ACKER

FOR YOUR TEAM OR EVENT

Mike Acker is an in-demand keynote speaker on effective communication, emotional intelligence, and transformational leadership. His work in coaching, writing, and speaking inspires audiences around the nation and the globe. His first book, Speak With No Fear, achieved the status of the highest-ranking book on overcoming nervousness in speaking.

He has worked with Adobe, Amazon, Microsoft, Oracle, INOApps, Dallas International School, US Federal Agencies, International Monetary Fund, and many others.

If you are interested in booking Mike Acker for a keynote presentation, workshop, or virtual program, please contact info@mikeacker.com or visit www.MikeAcker.com.

Past Engagements Include:

Explore The Public Speaking School and work personally with Mike Acker:

1-on-1 Coaching | Professional Online Course Curriculum | Monthly Mastermind Cohort

Create Confidence through Communication.

1. Overcome insecurity and anxiety.
2. Learn how to connect with others.
3. Develop Executive Presence.

Don't wait: set up a free consultation:
https://advance.as.me/SWNF

(Available for individuals and teams)

ALSO BY MIKE ACKER

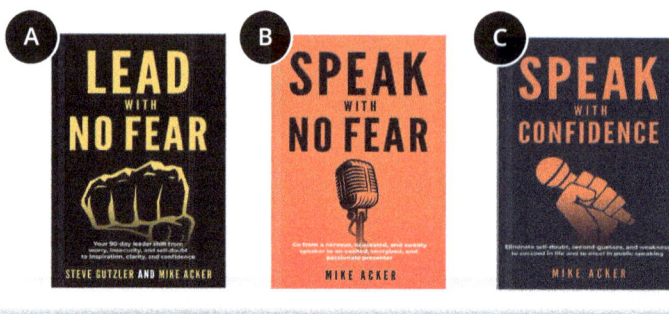

A — Lead with No Fear
In this conversational and action-oriented book, Steve Gutzler and Mike Acker present seven shifts to direct your leadership towards your desired destination: impact, influence, and inspiration.

B — Speak with No Fear
Speak With No Fear is the #1 globally highest-ranked book on overcoming the fear of speaking. Full of relatable anecdotes, executable tips, and plenty of laugh-out-loud moments, this book promises to teach you seven proven strategies to help you find your inner presenter.

C — Speak with Confidence
Don't just overcome nervousness; discover Mike Acker's proven framework for developing profound confidence to eliminate self-doubt, second-guessing, and weak presence to excel in public speaking and succeed in life.

D — Write to Speak
A simple guide to creating content that connects you with your audience. Readers will learn a repeatable system that works for novice and experienced speakers.

E — Connect through Emotional Intelligence
In *Connect through Emotional Intelligence*, you will learn to master yourself, avoid disconnection with others, and bridge gaps through increasing your understanding and applying new principles. Increasing your emotional intelligence will improve your relationships, your leadership, and your life.

www.ingramcontent.com/pod-product-compliance
Lightning Source LLC
Chambersburg PA
CBHW061109070526
44579CB00012B/188